Be sure to look for these titles in the *Go Parents!* series:

Teaching Your Children Good Manners will help make teaching your children the basics of good manners an entertaining and (relatively) painless experience.

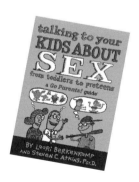

Talking to Your Kids About Sex: From Toddlers to Preteens takes a common-sense, practical approach to helping parents talk to children of a variety of ages and developmental levels about a topic that makes many people uncomfortable.

(August 2002)

"Whether your child licks a frozen flagpole or plays pattycake with a cactus, this book has the solution. *"Mom, the Toilet's Clogged!" Kid Disasters and How to Fix Them* is a great gift for any parent, grandparent or person with a retainer stuck in the garbage disposer."

—Tim Bete
Award-winning humor columnist and father of three

". . . *Kid Disasters and How to Fix Them* is a handy-dandy compendium for anyone, especially those with kids in residence. Author Lauri Berkenkamp offers no-nonsense solutions to a myriad of child-related catastrophes. Her directions are clear and her remedies call for items found at home such as peanut butter, scissors and white glue. Readers with fly-paper minds will delight in the off-beat facts sprinkled throughout the book. Zippy illustrations combined with Berkenkamp's solid, chatty advice makes this book a winner."

—Nancy Nash-Cummings
Nationally syndicated columnist ("Ask Ann and Nan")
and co-author of *Clean It, Find It, Fix It.*

Kid Disasters
and How to Fix Them
a *Go Parents!* guide™

Nomad Press
A division of Nomad Communications
10 9 8 7 6 5 4 3 2 1
Copyright © 2002 Nomad Communications

ISBN 0-9659258-4-6

Questions regarding the ordering of this book should be addressed to
The Independent Publishers Group
814 N. Franklin St.
Chicago, IL 60610

Cover artwork and interior illustrations by Charles Woglom, Big Hed Designs
Design by Bruce Leasure and David Morin
Edited by Susan Hale and Anna Typrowicz

Nomad Press, PO Box 875, Norwich, VT 05055

To John and Ginna, who can fix anything.

—LB

Table of Contents

Section 1   Page 3

I Told You Not to Touch That: Body-related Predicaments

Section 2   Page 21

Don't Flush! Plumbing and Appliance Disasters

Section 3   Page 39

What's That on the Rug? Interior Household Destruction

Section 4   Page 57

What Did You Do to That Window?
When Bad Things Happen Outside

Be Prepared   Page 68

A Few Items to Keep Handy

Just Say Cheese and Don't Turn Your Head

It's school picture day, and as your son sits down to breakfast, you notice he has something stuck to his head, making his hair puff up like a skunk's tail. It's really not his best look.

"Oh, that's gum," he says, patting his hair and turning sideways to show you how it's also stuck to his cheek and ear. "I slept on it by accident. You should see my pillow."

As you assess the damage you wonder if the school photographer has ever actually refused to take a child's photo before. You debate whether to look for the scissors now, or capture the moment on film. This will certainly be a picture to remember.

Sound familiar? Don't worry—help is at hand. *"Mom, the Toilet's Clogged!" Kid Disasters and How to Fix Them* takes on common and not-so-common kid-related disasters, and provides hands-on, common-sense solutions that really work. This book covers everyday traumas in detail, from clogged toilets to heads stuck in between stair railings, complete with solutions, helpful hints, and interesting bits of information that you never thought you'd need—until you became a parent.

How to Use This Book

This book should be used as a guide; the disasters related in it have actually happened and certainly will again. The solutions are based on advice from qualified professionals and seasoned parents, and acknowledge that while coping with kid-related disasters may drive you nuts, they can also make you laugh—eventually.

The book is divided into sections that address related kid disasters. Has your son superglued his hands together or stuck gum in his hair? Look in Section 1: **I Told You Not to Touch That** for solutions to these and other body-related dilemmas. Plumbing problems? Section 2: **Don't Flush!** addresses plumbing and appliance disasters from overflowing toilets to jammed garbage disposals. Section 3: **What's That on the Rug?** offers aid to interior house disasters ranging from carpet stains to holes in drywall, and Section 4: **What Did You Do to That Window?** takes care of exterior disasters, from broken windows to dead car batteries.

And while you're scrubbing marker off the walls or sweeping up the glass from that broken window, remember that while every day as a parent brings new opportunities for disaster, this book will help prepare you for whatever comes up, goes down, or gets stuck.

Section 1:

i Told You NOT to TOUCH That!

A Brush with Cactus Spines

You're at the local plant and garden center picking up some
mulch. Your children ask if they can go look in the greenhouse
where the exotic plants are kept. "Sure," you reply, half listening,
intent on making mulch decisions. After all, how much trouble
could they get into in there? It's just a bunch of plants, for
heaven's sake.

Plenty of trouble, it turns out. While you're at the checkout your
daughter comes up to you, whimpering, "I had a little accident
with a cactus," and shows you hundreds of feathery prickers
coating the back of her hand. You try not to wince, and mentally
switch gears from an afternoon of happy mulching to hours of
plucking (you) and crying (her).

Here's What You Need

Cellophane tape

Tweezers

White household glue

Antiseptic

Warm water

Here's What to Do

If the spines are big enough to see, try gently using cellophane tape to lift them off. If they are in too deep to pull off with tape, you should be able to remove them with a pair of tweezers. Don't pick at them with a needle—it can cause infections and kids hate it. You need to be careful in any case not to break off the spine under the skin, since this too can cause infection.

Many cacti, especially the kind sold in plant stores, have spines that are practically invisible, and are very difficult to remove since you can't see them to pluck them. And it's impossible to pluck them all if you're talking about hundreds. Cover the affected area with a thick coat of white household glue and let it dry. Peel it carefully off the skin and the cactus spines will come off, as well. Repeat the whole process as necessary.

Put antiseptic on any puncture wounds, and keep an eye out for redness or swelling that might indicate infection from fungus on the spines.

Interesting Tip

These methods also work for less exotic pricker incidents like falling into raspberry or rose bushes or grabbing crab grass, as well as for just your basic splinter. If the splinter is completely below the surface and doesn't come out with tweezers, tape, or glue, try soaking the affected area in warm water three or four times a day for five minutes or so. Usually the splinter will swell and surface on its own.

Bean up the Nose

You and your kids are at the grocery store doing some shopping. You're in the coffee aisle when you remember that you need toilet paper, which is back in aisle three. You ask your son to fill a bag with coffee and wait for you with the cart while you run back. Upon your return, you notice your son snuffling like a rabbit while trying hard to stay out of your line of vision. He finally turns to you with a strange look on his face, and says, "I was putting coffee beans in my nose and then shooting them out, but now one's stuck." You wonder again why you don't try harder to go shopping at night, alone, while they are all asleep.

Here's What to Do

Remember that the biggest danger with something up a nose is that your retrieval method will push it farther in. If you can't see the bean, or if it's causing pain, you should probably call the doctor and let him or her pull it out.

With that said, if the bean (or other object) is close to the surface and clearly visible, the easiest method to extract it is to hold one finger over the other nostril, and blow. Encourage your child to breathe through his mouth in between nose blows so that the bean doesn't get sucked farther up his nose.

If you can see the bean but your fingers are too big to pluck it out, very carefully try to remove the bean with a pair of fine tweezers.

If the bean isn't visible but it's close enough to the opening and large enough that you can feel it by gently pressing on your son's nose, gently rub in a downward motion from the bridge of the nose to the nostril, so the bean works its way down the nostril far enough to try the nose-blow method. If this hurts too much, stop and call the doctor.

And the Survey Says ...

This sounds like a ridiculous problem, but four out of five parents surveyed said that one of their children had stuck a foreign object in either his or her nose or ear and had to have it retrieved. Some of these objects included rocks, hair beads, lettuce, Fruit Loops, and rice. Go figure.

Bug in the Ear

You're cooking up dinner over a can of Sterno on your family camping trip when suddenly your daughter runs up and says, "Yuck! A moth flew in my ear." You try not to shudder in front of her, and tell her to shake her head really hard. No luck. She's crying, you're repulsed. This was not in the camper's manual. What do you do?

Here's What You Need

Flashlight

Blanket *(if no dark room available)*

Towel

Water bottle or other pourable container

Warm water

Here's What to Do

Amazing But True Solution: Find a location that can be made completely dark, such as a closet, bathroom, or even under a blanket or in a sleeping bag. Turn off all the lights and shine a flashlight directly into her ear. The moth may fly out toward the flashlight. Try this method before you move on to the alternative, which is to flood your child's ear with water—after repeated floodings the moth may be too wet to move.

Alternative: Have your daughter sit down and tilt her head so that the affected ear is facing up. Put a towel over her shoulder so she isn't soaked, then gently flood the ear with warm water until the moth floats out. If it doesn't float out the first time, try again. If it doesn't appear after repeated floodings, it's time to call the doctor. Do NOT stick anything in your daughter's ear to poke, pick, or prod it out.

Note: If you don't have water handy, flooding the ear with mineral oil will kill the bug, as well. However, mineral oil can cause insects to become briefly more active, which may freak out your child even more.

Moths Really Are Lightheaded

Moths are positively phototactic, which means they automatically move to sources of light; cockroaches, on the other hand, are negatively phototactic and scurry away from light sources. While there are no definitive answers for this phenomenon, some scientists theorize that because moths are oriented up and down, they use the moon as their primary reference point for navigation. Artificial light serves as a substitute "moon" for them and leads to disorientation when they reach the light source.

Head Stuck Between Railings

You're at the mall, having a great shopping expedition. You and your son are upstairs on the second floor when you decide to take in the view. You lean on the metal railing, enjoying the scene of shoppers scurrying around below. Suddenly, your son says, "Mom, my head's stuck." He has pushed his head through the bars of the railing and now can't get it out again. A small crowd surrounds you, offering advice. "Put petroleum jelly on his ears." "Dish soap works like a charm." "You're going to need a welder—I've seen it a hundred times."

Here's What to Do

Railings are usually tapered from top to bottom, meaning that the gap between them shrinks as they extend toward the ground. Often when kids push their heads through railings, they do so by leaning with their heads against the rails and sliding through. The momentum can make them lean forward and down—getting stuck because they try to pull their heads out at a lower spot than they pushed them through. Help your son bring his head up as 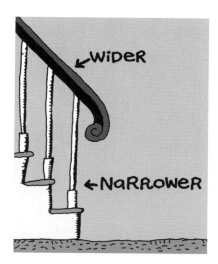 high between the railings as possible, and gently ease his head back through at the highest point.

If the railing isn't tapered, it's likely that your son is trying to pull his head out between the railings at a different angle than he pushed it through. Make sure he tilts his head so that it is upright and he's looking straight across when passing back through—this will help him avoid squishing his ears against the railings.

You won't need lubricants of any kind to get his head out, unless it helps him psychologically to have his head greased up for removal.

Interesting Fact

There's something about a kid with his head stuck in a railing that brings out the sideline coach in people. Ignore all of the fabulous suggestions you'll be getting from spectators—especially the ones that will scare him, like using a blowtorch. Keep him as calm as possible, and remember that unless he's a magician, if his head went in it will come out.

Gum In Hair

You're driving in the car with a load of gum–chewing children, their small jaws working overtime to the music on the radio. You're enjoying the quiet that only a pack of Bubble Yum can bring, when one kid in the back of the car says, "Hey, let's have a bubble blowing contest!"

Before you can say a word, his half–blown bubble accidentally shoots out of his mouth directly into the back of your daughter's head. The wad is stuck fast, and you spend the rest of the car ride home wondering how your daughter might look with a crew cut.

Here's What You Need

Peanut butter

Ice cubes

Here's What to Do

Don't let her yank on it, finger it, or try to pull it out by herself, especially if it's fresh. It'll just make the gum stringy and get it on your car upholstery or her clothes. When you get home, pull out the peanut butter. Coat the entire glob of gum with peanut butter and massage it into the gum. The oil in the peanut butter will start to dissolve the resins in the gum, and you can slowly comb out the gum chunks. This will take patience and your daughter will smell like peanuts for the rest of the day, but her hair will be saved.

Alternative: You can freeze the gum by rubbing ice cubes on the wad until it is brittle enough to break off. Please note that this takes quite a long time, and most people using the ice method eventually give up and cut out the wad with scissors.

Interesting Fact

Gum is made up of a combination of sugar, gum base, corn syrup, flavoring, softeners, and coloring. Most gum bases are synthetic (meaning plastic), but may also contain natural forms of latex. Since most of these ingredients are indigestible, any gum your kids swallow won't stay in their stomachs for more than a couple of days—not seven years, regardless of what your best friend told you when you were seven.

Superglued Hands

Your son and his friend have been happily occupied in his room for almost an hour. At first you enjoy the peace and quiet, but the occasional muffled bursts of laughter eventually make you suspicious. You're heading upstairs to find out just what's so funny, when they burst out of your son's bedroom with horrified looks on their faces. Your son's friend reaches out to you with both hands together as if he's praying and says, "I superglued my hands together and it really works!" Do you send him home and pretend you didn't notice, or do you try to fix this one yourself?

Here's What You Need

Nail polish remover

Cotton balls

Here's What to Do

Superglue is a cyanoacrylate adhesive designed to bind to nonporous material. It sets by contact with moisture so a slightly grimy child's hand is an ideal bonding medium.

The easiest way to counteract the effects of superglue is to use nail polish remover or acetone. Soak a cotton ball with polish remover and apply liberally to the affected area. Since both of his palms are entirely glued together, you'll have to squeeze polish remover from the cotton ball into the crevices between his hands. The glue will start to de-bond on contact. Make sure he doesn't pull his hands apart, since he may damage his skin, and it'll hurt. Rather, have him slide his hands back and forth as he feels the glue debonding. Eventually his hands will come apart. Remember to be careful where you perform the superglue-ectomy. Acetone can be very corrosive to counter-tops or other surfaces.

If you don't have nail polish remover, soak his hands in warm, soapy water. This method takes time, but will work eventually.

Interesting Fact

Many doctors now use a medical version of super-glue instead of traditional sutures to close skin wounds, usually eliminating the need for needle-injected anesthetic. Needle-phobic people everywhere, rejoice!

Tongue Stuck to Freezer

You're at the grocery store, maneuvering your overloaded cart down the frozen food aisle. Your kids are getting restless and whiny, so to distract them you assign them each a mission: Number 1, get french fries. Number 2: waffles. Number 3: frozen juice. Numbers 1 and 2 come back promptly, mission accomplished. But Number 3 is still leaning into the freezer. You trundle your cart down to see what's keeping her and discover that she's not just leaning into the frozen juice compartment—she's licked it and now her tongue is securely attached to one of the shelves. You wonder if it's just you, or do these things ever happen to other, normal families?

Here's What You Need

Warm water

Table salt

Here's What to Do

Tell your daughter NOT to yank her tongue off the freezer: it'll hurt and she'll take off some skin. Instead, you can either go to the seasonings aisle, get some salt and sprinkle it around her tongue, which will melt it enough to pull her tongue away, or you can use a small amount of warm water to release her tongue.

If you don't have warm water, you can melt the area by breathing warm air on it, but this will take time and patience, and it depends on how close you want to get your mouth to either your daughter's tongue OR the grocery store freezer.

Be aware that if you pour water on the area, your daughter should lift off her tongue immediately; otherwise, she'll just get stuck again since the water will quickly freeze. Also remember to keep damp body parts away from the freezer while performing the tongue-ectomy, as there is the chance that resting a wet hand on the rim of the freezer will make it stick, too.

Interesting Fact

This type of kid disaster happens frequently on school playgrounds in winter. Apparently metal slides are irresistible to young children, as many a salt– or warm water–wielding school nurse will attest.

Petroleum Jelly in Hair

Your son has decided to be a vampire for Halloween. He disappears upstairs to finish putting on his costume, while you wait with camera and candy bag in hand. He walks down the stairs with requisite black cape and fanged face, but you notice that his head seems exceptionally shiny. "It's Vaseline®," he explains, patting his hair, then trailing his greasy hand on the wall. "All the vampires wear it."

Later that night, after all the soap and shampoo you own has been magically repelled by the goo coating his hair, you wonder how he'll look with a shaved head. You try to remember what you did with the dog clippers.

Here's What to Do

Take a paper towel and blot as much of the petroleum jelly from his hair as possible. Don't rub, or you'll just mat his hair.

Shake cornstarch or cornmeal powder on his hair and pat it in, making sure his whole head is covered with a light coating, similar to how you'd prepare oven-fried chicken. Do not use talcum powder, because it's harmful to the lungs if inhaled.

Put him in a warm—not hot—shower, and apply shampoo. Do not use the kind of shampoo that also contains conditioner. The cornstarch or cornmeal powder that you've patted onto your son's hair will bind with the petroleum jelly and help the shampoo carry it out of his hair.

Shampoo his head twice to make sure all of the petroleum jelly and powder are out of his hair. Let his hair air dry. If it looks like there are still traces of petroleum jelly in his hair, do another cornstarch—shampoo treatment.

Interesting Fact

Cornstarch is very fine flour made from the heart, or endosperm, of the corn kernel. It is most often used as a thickening agent in food recipes. It also makes a great homemade version of Silly Putty® when mixed with white glue.

Section 2:
DON'T FLUSH!

Dishwasher Overflowing with Suds

You need to run out to the store, so you make a deal with your kids: they can stay at home and finish watching their show IF they clean the kitchen for you while you're gone. As you walk around the store blissfully unencumbered, you're thinking you made a pretty savvy deal. And then you get home and are greeted at the front door by your daughter who yells, "Mom! Come quick! The dishwasher has gone nuts and soap suds are moving into the family room!" Calgon®, take you away.

Here's What You Need

1 cup table salt OR
1 cup white vinegar

Damp mop

Here's What to Do

Unless there is something seriously wrong with your dishwasher (in which case, call a repair service), your kids probably put liquid dish soap in the automatic dish detergent dispenser. Confirm this with your kids before you do anything else.

Open the dishwasher and pour in one cup of table salt. Wait a minute or so, then turn the dishwasher on again for a couple of minutes. The salt will break down the suds inside the dishwasher,

 and you can then rewash all the dishes using automatic dish detergent. An alternative to the salt method is to use a cup of white vinegar. This will also dissolve the soap bubbles, and will clean the inside of your dishwasher, to boot.

As for the floor, you may not be able to stand it, but it's really easiest to clean up foamy suds after they've dissolved back into soap scum. Wade through the suds for now, enjoy your kitchen-sized bubble bath, and your kids can mop up the filmy residue with a slightly damp mop later.

Interesting Fact

If you have "soft" water, it's likely you'll have more suds spewing out of your dishwasher than if you have "hard" water. Soft water contains no minerals to inhibit the creation of soap bubbles, while hard water usually contains calcium and magnesium, which combine with soap and detergent to form a scum that doesn't dissolve in water. And you thought that ring around the tub in your kids' bathroom was dirt . . .

Food Explosion in the Microwave

Your son comes home from school and is ravenously hungry. It's slim pickings in the refrigerator, and his choices are leftover fish sticks, leftover stir fry, or leftover hard-boiled eggs. He goes for the eggs. He takes a bite, decides he doesn't like them cold, and sticks a couple in the microwave. Time: 1 minute. Press Start. Go.

Twenty seconds later the eggs explode and coat the entire interior of the microwave with a fine film of yellow and white. Your son doesn't notice. He's waiting for the "ding" to say the microwave's done. The eggs cook and cook, hardening on to the walls and ceiling of the microwave like a coat of smelly paint.

Ding! One minute's up. Your son opens the microwave door and asks, "Hey, where're my eggs?"

Here's What to Do

At this point in their cooking cycle, the eggs are probably more like stucco than food. Brush out any pieces of shell or egg that aren't glued to the interior of the microwave.

Pour a cup of white vinegar into a microwave-safe, open container and put it in the center of the microwave. Turn it on full power for 2 to 3 minutes. The vinegar will boil and steam off much of the stuccoed egg from the walls and ceiling and will get rid of the sulphur smell.

Take out the vinegar and wipe down the walls with a warm, soapy cloth. Your microwave should be egg-free, and probably cleaner than it's been in a while. If you still have stuff stuck to the walls, repeat the process.

Interesting Fact

Contrary to what all your friends told you in eighth grade, microwave ovens don't cook things from the inside out. Rather, the electromagnetic radiation emitted by microwave ovens is at exactly the right wavelength to excite water molecules—and when water molecules are excited, they heat up. Since most food contains water of varying amounts, the microwaves heat up the water inside the food. Microwaves can pass through plastic and glass, but they don't penetrate very deeply into the food itself, which is why if you try to heat up something very frozen or very big it'll often be hot on the outside and still frozen in the middle.

Crayon in the Dryer

You're happily doing your daily mountain of laundry, and you've been flipping loads from washer to dryer with remarkable efficiency. As you reach into the dryer to remove the last load, you discover that everything in it is smeared with greasy streaks of pink, violet, and brown crayon. One of your kids threw their clothes in the laundry hamper with crayons in the pockets, and despite your obsession with checking pockets for lurking disaster, this one managed to get by you. Bummer.

Here's What You Need

Paper towels

WD-40®

Liquid dish soap

Baking soda

Here's What to Do

Before you do anything else, check your washer to make sure little chunks of crayon didn't break off during the wash cycle. Spray a little WD-40® on the washer drum and then run a quick empty load to make sure your washer is crayon-free. Then check the dryer to make sure chunks or streaks of crayon are not melted to the drum. If so, scrape these off and remove. Spray a fine mist of WD-40® on a cloth and wipe down the interior to clean away any crayon residue, then wash the drum with warm soapy water to remove any remaining WD-40®. It's a good idea to run a load of dry rags through the dryer as a test before adding any clothes you value.

Go through the load of clothes and scrape off any crayon that may be thickly lumped on the fabric. Place each article of clothing on some paper towels and spray the stain with WD-40® on both sides of the fabric.

Soak the load of clothes in hot water with a tablespoon of dish soap and one-half cup baking soda for about 10 minutes. You may need to make a paste of baking soda and soap for stubborn or larger streaks.

Wash in a short cycle and rinse. If color remains, spot treat with bleach or color remover that's safe for your fabric.

> ## *Interesting Fact*
>
> *Crayons are made of a combination of paraffin wax, stearic acid, and color pigment, and melt at approximately 105 degrees Fahrenheit. According to the 2000 Crayola® Color Census, America's favorite crayon color is blue—plain blue. Does anyone ever vote for burnt sienna?*

Jammed Garbage Disposer

You've just finished dinner and your children are helping to clean up the kitchen. There is the usual squabbling over who has to clear the table and who has to load the dishwasher, and in the ensuing commotion your son suddenly realizes that his orthodontic retainer is missing. He thinks for a minute, and just as he says, "I think I might have left it on my plate," you hear a horrible grinding sound and then a hum coming from the disposer. You flip off the switch and peer in. There, among the remains of the meatloaf and salad, is his retainer, stuck fast in the blades. This was one expensive dinner.

Here's What You Need

Needlenose pliers

Allen wrench

Broom handle or other sturdy stick

Here's What to Do

Make sure you disconnect the disposer from its power source before trying to retrieve the retainer. Unplug it or break the connection at the circuit breaker or fuse box.

When you're sure the power to the disposer is definitely off, try to reach your hand or some needlenose pliers down in to pull out the retainer. If it's stuck underneath the blades, you'll have to move the blades themselves to get it free.

Most disposers come with an Allen wrench (a hexagonal metal rod with the end bent at a 45-degree angle) and have a hexagonal port in the center of the bottom of the unit, underneath the sink. If you have bikes and a bike repair kit, you're likely to have an Allen wrench somewhere in the house, even if the one for your disposer is missing.

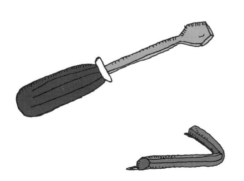

Take the wrench and insert it into the opening on the bottom of the disposer. When you turn the wrench back and forth you'll be wiggling the masher plate, which should help unjam the retainer from the blades. Then reach in from above and pull out the retainer.

If your disposer doesn't have the Allen-wrench port in the bottom, take a broom handle, stick it down into the disposer, and pry on one of the masher blades to force the plate to move. Be aware that this method can be pretty hard on the retainer, but usually is effective in getting the blades to move.

When you've retrieved the retainer (or what's left of it), and the blades of the disposer turn freely, check to make sure that the disposer is reset—there is a circuit breaker button on the lower side of the unit that will have popped out if it overloaded. Push the red reset button back in, plug in the disposer unit again, and test the disposer.

Interesting Tip

You should never run hot water while using a disposer. The hot water will melt grease that can then congeal in your pipes. Instead, use cold water so that the solid grease moves all the way to the sewage system. You should also never put Metamucil® down your disposer or in the sink. They're not kidding when they say it's a bulking agent, as your plumber will attest when he sends you his bill.

Mysterious Toilet Clog

You're busy picking up random toys around the house when you hear the words you dread: "Mom, the toilet's clogged!"

Your six-year-old has been in the bathroom. What appears to be about three rolls' worth of toilet paper is soggily floating in the brimming bowl. He looks blankly at you, says, "What? I had to go the bathroom," and wisely leaves the room. You're left alone with a rapidly rising toilet—any false moves on your part and what's in the bowl will be on the floor and out in the hall before you can say, "E. coli."

Here's What to Do

Part 1: Plunging and Augering

Put on a pair of rubber gloves—this could get messy. If the water is up to the rim of the toilet you'll need to bail some out in order to plunge the clog without sloshing toilet water all over the bathroom floor. Bail water into a bucket until there is still enough water in the bowl to cover the plunger cup, but not enough that it will spill over when the plunger is in the toilet.

Insert the plunger at an angle so there is no air trapped under the cup, and pump up and down 20 times, then pull it away sharply on the last stroke. The clog should be pushed through by the force of the plunger.

Take the lid off the tank on the back of the toilet. Do a test flush to see if the clog has been pushed completely through the toilet and into your pipes. If the water in the bowl rises rapidly and looks like it's going over the top, you'll be able to grab the weighted ball in the tank quickly to prevent a flood. Hold onto the ball until the toilet stops running and get ready to try again.

Plunge again and do another test flush. If water is still not going through the pipes, you may need to use a toilet auger (or toilet snake), a long bendy metal extender that you can work down into the pipes of your toilet. Place the padded end of the auger into the toilet bowl and work it into the toilet trap by turning it clockwise. Keep turning the auger until you reach the clog, and continue turning it as you remove the auger from the toilet. This will help push it through the pipes and down.

Part 2: Removing the Toilet

You've been in the bathroom for an hour, first plunging, then augering, now swearing and plunging and augering, but the toilet that was clogged then is still clogged now. You call the perpetrator back into the bathroom and under pressure he confesses that his bendable Spiderman action figure may have accidentally slipped out of his hand and may have ended up in the toilet and may have been flushed because he didn't want to stick his hand in to pull it out. Your clog: Spiderman. Your job: Spiderman rescue.

This job is easier than it sounds—it just takes time, patience, and a strong back.

1 Make sure to collect all of the tools and supplies before starting this project—especially the new wax ring.

2 Shut off the water supply to the toilet at the valve (the small metal valve usually on the floor or the wall attached to the toilet). Drain the tank by flushing the toilet—and since it's clogged, be ready to hold the weighted ball to avoid overflowing the bowl again. Bail and plunge any water left in the bowl, and put a towel on the floor behind the toilet to help mop up future spillage.

3 Take out the water supply line from the tank by unscrewing the fitting that threads onto the bottom of the tank. Remove the bolts from the inside of the tank and take the tank off the bowl.

4 Remove the bolts holding the toilet to the floor. They are usually covered with plastic caps, which can be popped off.

5 When everything attaching the toilet to the floor has been removed, lift the bowl straight up. You may need two people for this part. There is a wax ring underneath the toilet, which may make it stick, so be prepared for resistance.

6 If possible, take the toilet outside to remove the clog from underneath. Alternatively, place the toilet on towels or newspaper or at least someplace where you can deal with raw sewage leaks.

7 Remove Spiderman. Throw him away or clean him in a bleach solution.

8 Pull off all traces of the old wax ring, and place a new wax ring around the drain opening on the floor. The ring keeps the toilet level and creates a water-tight seal.

9 Replace the toilet by reversing the process.

Interesting Fact

The standard size of a sheet of toilet paper is 4.5 inches by 4.5 inches, although some toilet paper manufacturers skimp on size and produce sheets as small as 3.8 inches. The average consumer uses 57 sheets of toilet paper a day, or 20,805 sheets annually, and it takes an average of five days to use a single roll of toilet paper. If you have kids, of course, all usage statistics are meaningless.

Treasure Down the Sink

Your daughter just got contact lenses, and decides to try putting them in by herself for the very first time. She leans over the sink to get closer to the mirror, puts the slippery lens on the tip of her finger, opens her eye wide—and blinks the lens into the sink, right down the drain. You are alerted that there might be a problem by the hysterical screaming emanating from the upstairs bathroom. You rush upstairs to find her squinting at you, pointing to the sink and then back at her eye. You get the picture.

Here's What You Need

Bucket

Adjustable wrench or pipe wrench

Here's What to Do

Immediately turn off the faucet if it's running.

You may have the kind of sink with a remov-
able stopper. While hard objects such as
teeth, Legos, beads, and earrings tend to
wash down into the trap, softer or lighter
items such as contact lenses will often stick
to the stopper before getting washed away.
Pull the stopper out of the sink and check to
see if the contact has adhered to it before
moving on to Plan B: removing the sink trap.

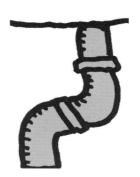

The sink trap is the s-shaped curve just below the bowl, where
most objects washed down the drain end up.

Put a bucket under the sink to
catch any water that might be in
the trap. Then loosen the two
couplings of the sink trap. You
may be able to unscrew them by
hand; otherwise, use a pipe
wrench. Take the trap and pour
the contents into a bowl. You
may find little bits of dirt or other
disgusting stuff, but the contact
lens should be there. After
retrieving the lens, fit the sink
trap back on the two pieces of
pipe and screw the couplings
until they are tight. Be careful not
to overtighten the couplings,
especially if they are PVC—
cracks will mean leaks.

Interesting Fact

*The human ear can tolerate
sounds at up to about 120
decibels. To put this in per-
spective, a soft whisper
measures 30 decibels, while
an alarm clock ringing at 2
feet away is approximately
80 decibels. Your daughter's
hysterical screaming, if done
directly into your ear, will
most likely reach up to 120
decibels, which is loud
enough to cause immediate
damage.*

Section 3:

What's that on the RUG?

Loose Door Hinges

Your son is swinging again—he has this annoying habit of opening doors, grabbing on to both doorknobs at once, and then hanging on them while swinging back and forth. You open your mouth to say, "I have told you a million times that you're going to break the door!" when it actually does break. The hinges pull slightly out of the frame, and the door lists drunkenly to one side. You were never great at shop class, so now what?

Here's What You Need

White glue or wood glue

Wooden toothpicks or golf tees

Sandpaper

Wood file or rasp

Small drill or awl

Screwdriver

Here's What to Do

What's happened is that the weight of your son hanging on the knobs has stripped the wood screws holding the hinges in the wood of the frame. You'll need to remove the hinges and reset the screws in the wood.

Take the door off the frame by tapping the pins out of the hinges.

Unscrew the hinges from the frame. You'll probably see where the screw has pulled away from the wood, leaving a bigger hole than the screw can fill. You need to plug that hole so the screws are biting in to solid wood once again.

The easiest way to do this is to put white glue or wood glue into each screw hole and either fill it with wooden toothpicks or tap in a golf tee until the hole is completely filled. Wipe off any excess glue and wait for it to dry.

If any toothpick or golf tee ends are sticking out, cut them off and sand the filled hole to make sure it's smooth—otherwise, the hinge plate won't rest flush against the frame.

Use a small drill or awl to make a starter hole in the hole you've plugged, then replace the hinge plate and the screws.

Line up the door hinges with the frame hinge plates, and tap the pins back in. You may need to work the pins a bit to get them back in the whole way.

Interesting Fact

The remains of a 1.8-million-year-old Homo Erectus from Kenya's Olduvai Gorge indicate that the world's oldest humans used toothpicks to clean their teeth in a manner very similar to how people use them today.

Broken Objets d'Art

It happens just like that episode of the Brady Bunch. Your kids are tossing a ball in the living room, and just as you open your mouth to say, "Don't play ball in the house!" it deflects off your son's hand and knocks over the porcelain vase your Aunt Edna gave you that you were planning to take to the Antiques Roadshow. The vase cracks into several pieces, and your hopes for hidden riches are crushed. Can this vase be saved?

Here's What You Need

Masking tape

Modeling clay or playdough

Ceramic glue

Here's What to Do

Get some masking tape and stick the broken pieces of vase on the tape to help you keep track of them. Find some modeling clay, playdough, or other doughy substance so you can temporarily reattach the broken pieces to see how they should all fit together.

When you've figured out how all the pieces go together, carefully take the vase apart, remove the clay, and lay out the pieces in order.

You're ready to glue, but remember that you'll need to use ceramic glue to reattach the pieces, as porcelain is very porous, and regular adhesives such as all-purpose glue or even superglue won't hold for long.

Glue each piece of the vase back together, if possible starting at the bottom and working your way up, depending on the breakage. If you can reach your hand into the vase, use masking tape along the crack so that the tape acts as a clamp while you glue the seams back together. Note that if you can see cracks in the vase while you're gluing, you'll see cracks later, too.

While the vase will no longer be watertight it will at least look pretty on the shelf.

Interesting Fact

The Brady Bunch television show filmed only 117 original episodes, and ran for 5 seasons, from 1969 to 1974, before going into syndication where Carol, Mike, and their kids still live today in a modified ranch with Astroturf®.

Broken Zipper

Your daughter bugged you for weeks to get her a new winter coat—and not just any winter coat, but the unbelievably expensive, microfiber, NASA-endorsed coat, which she assures you is guaranteed to make her smarter, faster, and an all-around better kid. So you relent, spend more money on her coat than your entire winter wardrobe, and bask in the glow of being the world's best parent. Until the next day, when she tells you the zipper broke, and you discover that all sales are final.

Here's What You Need

Manicure scissors

Bar of soap or candle

Needlenose pliers

Needle

Strong thread

Optional: Staple gun

Here's What to Do

First check to make sure the zipper isn't just sticky or has threads stuck in the teeth. If you find some stuck threads, cut them with manicure scissors (or the smallest scissors you can find) where they enter the slider. Pull them through to free the slider. Rub a bar of soap or a candle on the teeth and pull the slider up and down to make the zipper work more easily.

If the zipper has unmeshed, and you have a gap, follow these steps to fix it:

1 Remove the stop at the bottom of the zipper. You'll need a pair of needlenose pliers to do this. Grasp the stop with the pliers and work it out of the fabric slowly, making sure you don't rip the fabric around it. Be patient and it will come out.

2 Move the slider down the zipper, match up both sides of the zipper and run the slider back up, removing the gap.

3 Zip up the zipper completely and make sure that the fabric is aligned properly on both sides—you don't want one side longer than the other.

4 Create a new stop. You can make a new one by sewing a few stitches with strong, heavy thread (a cotton-polyester blend or 100% polyester) at the bottom of the zipper. Start from the back of the zipper so you don't have a mess in front and take two or three stitches across the bottom of the zipper. You want just enough thread to stop the zipper without making it too bulky.

Another option for creating a stop on large zippers (or ones whose appearance you don't care about as much) is to use heavy-duty staples from a staple gun, bending the edges into the fabric on the back side. It's kind of a Frankenstein look, and the staples will cause holes in the fabric if removed, so be committed to the staple look before you actually do it.

Interesting Fact

In 1917, a man named Gideon Sundbach received a patent for a "hookless fastener," which is the first known patent for what we call the zipper.

Unpleasant Stain on Carpet, Part 1

It's your birthday, and all you want to do is sleep in past 6:30. You're snuggled under the covers, thoroughly enjoying the luxury of dozing through the chaos downstairs, when suddenly you sit up—what is all that noise down there? You hear muffled thuds, a thumping coming up the stairs, and then all of your children burst into your room with a tray for breakfast in bed, complete with Lucky Charms and grape juice—their personal favorites. It's adorable, and they almost make it to the bed before the one holding the juice trips over your shoe and flings the entire contents of the enormous glass across your wall-to-wall carpet. Happy Birthday!

Here's What You Need

Towels

Vacuum

Liquid dish soap

Spray bottle with tap water

Paper towels

Hydrogen peroxide (3%)

White vinegar

Here's What to Do

Leap out of bed and blot up as much grape juice as possible. Worry about getting the stain out of the towel(s) later. If you have a shop vac or a vacuum that can suck up liquids, use it to get up as much standing liquid as you can.

Mix about $1/4$ teaspoon of liquid dish soap (NOT automatic dishwasher detergent) with one quart of warm water and blot it on with a paper towel. Don't scrub it in, although you will be tempted to, because this will further set the stain into the carpet fibers. If this process is bringing out the spot, continue to blot on soapy liquid and blot up the stain, then rinse with tap water by spraying with a spray bottle, until it is gone. If you don't have a spray bottle, use a wet paper towel and alternate blotting with soap solution and plain water. When the stain is gone, spray lightly with plain water (or dab with plain water), cover with a pad of clean paper towels and weigh down the towels with a heavy object (like a dictionary or encyclopedia) to soak up excess moisture. Let dry.

If the stain isn't coming up, moisten the stained area with 3% hydrogen peroxide. (Moisten doesn't mean saturate—keep this in mind if you want your carpet to remain the same color.) Let it stand for one hour, then blot and repeat until the stain is gone. Don't rinse. Then cover the area with a pad of clean paper towels and weigh it down.

Now About That Towel . . .

You may be able to throw it immediately into the washing machine, put it through a warm cycle, and get rid of the stain, since it won't have had time to set. Otherwise, soak it for about 15 minutes in the same solution you used on the carpet, adding 1 tablespoon of white vinegar. Then rinse the towel in warm water. The stain should be gone, but if not, buy a new towel and use this one to wash your car.

Unpleasant Stain on Carpet, Part 2

It's the weekend, and everyone is puttering in and out of the house, doing his or her own thing. You're outside in the yard and you need something from your room. You go inside and as you head up the stairs, you catch a whiff of something both familiar and unpleasant. It smells kind of like dog poop up there. And you know why: at the top of the stairs, making their way to your son's bedroom, are perfect size 4 sneaker tracks, reeking to the rafters. Your son and your dog had a close encounter of the worst kind.

Here's What to Do

First, find the shoes, get them off your son, and throw them outside to deal with later (obviously). Find some gloves and hold your breath; you're going in.

You'll need to scrape up any solid poop off the carpet with a blunt knife or spoon. Get as much solid material off the carpet as possible without grinding it in.

Here's What You Need

Rubber gloves

Dull knife or spoon

Household ammonia

Tap water

Paper towels

Hydrogen peroxide (3%)

Neutralize the areas by making a spray-bottle solution of 1 tablespoon household ammonia and $1/2$ cup of water and spraying this on the stains. If you don't have a spray bottle, blot this solution on the mess with saturated paper towels. Blot, don't scrub, the areas and get up all of the remaining poop.

Mix a solution of $1/4$ teaspoon of dishwashing liquid (NOT automatic dishwasher detergent) to one quart of water, and saturate a paper towel with it. Blot it into each stain. If this is removing the stains, keep applying the soapy solution and blotting until they are all gone. Then rinse with tap water by spraying with a spray bottle or saturating with wet clean paper towels. Cover each area with a pad of clean paper towels and weigh them down with a heavy object. This will soak up the remaining water.

If the stains aren't coming out with the detergent solution, moisten (but don't soak) the area with 3% hydrogen peroxide. Let this stand for about an hour, then blot it up and repeat if you need to. You don't need to rinse out the hydrogen peroxide. When the stains are gone, cover the area with a pad of clean paper towels and weigh them down to soak up the remaining liquid.

Interesting Fact

Dog poop isn't the only protein stain that should come out with the above process. You can also remove stains caused by baby food or formula, blood, deodorant, egg white, gelatin, urine, vomit, beef or chicken soup, and sherbet. Generally speaking, if it has protein in it, this will beat it.

Small Hole in the Drywall
(Your Daughter Has Reached Adolescence)

You and your daughter have a small argument and she stomps off to her room. You hear her door slam, then open, then slam, then open—and then a kind of a crunch. You go upstairs to see what happened, and find her busy putting up a poster on her wall, just behind her door at about waist height.

"What's with the poster?" you ask. "I like it there," she says. You point out that it's hidden behind the door, upside down, and mighty low for optimal viewing. She cracks under the pressure and shows you the hole her doorknob made slamming into the wall. You bite back your anger—it's pretty clear how sorry she is—and tell her you'll fix it together. You are a good mother.

Here's What You Need

Scissors or utility knife

Spackling compound

Rough and medium-grit sandpaper

Damp sponge

Putty knife

Paint

Here's What to Do

Because a doorknob hole is usually small, you can patch it up with lightweight spackling compound that you can buy at any hardware or home improvement store. First, cut off any loose or frayed paper edges around the hole. Then roughen the edges you're going to fill with some rough sandpaper so that the spackling compound adheres better.

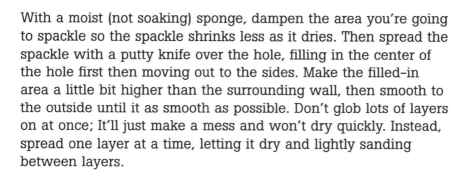

With a moist (not soaking) sponge, dampen the area you're going to spackle so the spackle shrinks less as it dries. Then spread the spackle with a putty knife over the hole, filling in the center of the hole first then moving out to the sides. Make the filled-in area a little bit higher than the surrounding wall, then smooth to the outside until it as smooth as possible. Don't glob lots of layers on at once; It'll just make a mess and won't dry quickly. Instead, spread one layer at a time, letting it dry and lightly sanding between layers.

Most spackle shrinks a bit when it dries, so you may need to put on another coat. If you do, scratch up the first coat so the second one adheres better, then repeat the above process. You may need to do this a few times to get the patched place completely smooth. Make sure you give the spackle adequate time to dry in between coats.

Finally, sand the patched area with medium-grit sandpaper and paint it.

Interesting Fact

Remember physics class, where you learned that Force = Mass x Acceleration? Well, here it is in action. The harder your daughter slams the door, the more force is exerted by the doorknob on the wall. If your daughter was really angry and the damage is extreme, please see Bigger Hole in the Drywall.

Bigger Hole in the Drywall
(Your Daughter is Stronger Than You Thought)

You and your daughter begin to repair the hole she made in her wall, but as you cut off the frayed wallboard you realize that it's really almost six inches' worth of drywall you'll have to patch up. You're glad that you raised such an assertive daughter (that's what you're going with right now, anyway), but realize that the spackle-alone plan isn't going to work here. You go to Plan B: the drywall patch.

Here's What You Need

Utility knife

Piece of drywall or wallboard

Putty knife

Spackling compound

Keyhole saw or other thin-bladed saw

Sandpaper

Paint

Here's What to Do

1 Use the keyhole saw to make the hole in the wall into a square or rectangle so you can make a patch more easily to fit it.

2 Cut a piece of drywall the same shape as the hole that is big enough to overlap the hole by one inch on every side.

3 Place the piece of cut drywall on a flat surface, shiny side down. Measure one inch from all sides and mark this line around the patch. This should form a shape the size of the hole in the wall.

4 Cut through the drywall patch along the marked line with a utility knife down to the bottom layer, but DO NOT cut through the bottom layer of paper.

5 Using a putty knife, remove the top layer of paper and core away the drywall down to the bottom layer of paper all around the outside of the patch.

6 Check to make sure the patch fits the hole and trim very carefully if necessary.

7 Put a thin layer of spackling compound on the edges of the hole, and on the wall around the hole, and place the patch into the hole.

8 Carefully work the paper edges into the spackling compound. Feather the edges of the spackling compound over the paper and smooth it out toward the walls. Let dry.

9 If necessary, sand lightly and apply a second coat of spackling compound to blend in the patch.

10 Paint the area and remind your daughter to vent her frustration with a pillow rather than her doorknob.

Permanent Marker Mayhem

You are downstairs reading the newspaper, enjoying some much-needed peace and quiet. Actually, it's too peaceful and quiet. Something's up. You call upstairs and your three-year-old daughter calls back, "Don't come up here!" Not the words you want to hear.

You take the stairs two at a time and discover just how much damage a toddler can do with a permanent marker and five minutes of free time.

Here's What You Need

Rubbing alcohol

Nail polish remover

Damp cloth

Scouring powder

Baby oil or cold cream

Shellac-based primer

Here's What to Do

First, the clothes: Keep in mind that the whole raison d'etre of a permanent marker is to be permanent, so you may not be able to get it all out. In fact, removing permanent marker from fabric is almost impossible, but you can try blotting it with either rubbing alcohol or nail polish remover until you can't get any more ink to lift off the fabric. Then launder as usual. This will likely lighten the stain, but probably not remove it entirely.

Next, the walls: Permanent ink usually penetrates quickly into porous materials such as wallpaper, plaster, or painted drywall. As soon as possible, wipe the stained area with a cloth dampened (not soaked) in rubbing alcohol or acetone (for example, nail polish remover). Pour some scouring powder onto a damp cloth and scrub the stain, then rinse with water, but be aware that this could alter the color of your walls. If you catch it quickly enough, you may be able to get the stain off the wall. If not, you may need to use a shellac-based primer, and repaint the area.

Finally, her face: The good news is that permanent marker on skin fades with time. The bad news is that a full beard and mustache isn't her best look. Oil-based skin care products, such as baby oil and cold cream, will help remove some of the marker. Time will take care of the rest, but your toddler will probably have a five-o-clock shadow for a few days.

Interesting Fact

Permanent markers use a solvent-based ink, which etches into the paper (or fabric, drywall, or upholstery) on contact. Some solvent-based inks are toxic, so it's a good idea to be careful—for many reasons—about keeping them lying around the house. Permanent markers are indelible, but not necessarily lightfast or even fade-resistant—which is good news if your child used them on his or her face.

Section 4:

WhAT DiD you DO to That WINDOW?

Hole in Screen

It's a lazy, hot summer day, and your daughter is idling in a chair next to the window. She is absently poking the tip of a pencil into the window screen. You walk by, say, "Don't do that, you'll make a hole in it," and keep going. She continues delicately poking a little here and a little there, and says, "No I won't. I'm being really careful."

An hour later, you pass the window again. Surprise—there's a hole in the screen, and your daughter and her pencil have mysteriously disappeared. You begin to regret your decision not to send her to sleepover camp, after all.

Here's What You Need

Screen patch kit or extra piece of screen

Paper clip

Nylon thread and a needle

Clear nail polish

Here's What to Do

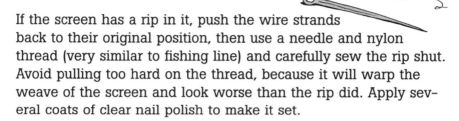

If the hole is a very small puncture, you can use an open paper clip to push the wire strands back to their original position and set them with clear nail polish.

If the screen has a rip in it, push the wire strands back to their original position, then use a needle and nylon thread (very similar to fishing line) and carefully sew the rip shut. Avoid pulling too hard on the thread, because it will warp the weave of the screen and look worse than the rip did. Apply several coats of clear nail polish to make it set.

If your daughter really went to town and poked a big hole, you're going to have to patch the screen. You can buy patch kits, which are really just little pieces of screen. Make sure you buy a patch kit made of the same material as your screen—fiberglass for fiberglass screen, metal for a metal screen.

Since the patch is never going to look exactly like the original screen, it's a good idea to trim the hole in the screen so the edges are straight. This will help to make the patch look as tidy as possible.

Cut the piece of patch about an inch wider than the hole. Unweave the edges of the patch just a bit by pulling out one or two wires around the edge, then bend up the edges of the remaining longer wires about 90 degrees.

Push the patch onto the screen so that the edges push through the screen, then gently flatten down the wires on the other side.

Broken Window Pane

You're out in the yard, raking leaves, while your kids fool around with an old set of golf clubs. You watch them practice swinging and just as you're assessing their chances at beating Tiger Woods in oh, twenty years, your daughter acciden-tally hits a rock with one of the clubs. Nice shot, but hooked left. The rock arcs through the air and out of sight toward the garage. You hear the tinkle of broken glass and realize that your daughter's golf career has gotten off to a shaky start—she just broke one of the garage windows.

Here's What You Need

A new pane of glass 1/16" smaller than the window frame

Chisel

Putty knife

Points (*small, wedge-shaped nails to secure the window*)

Hammer

Paint

Here's What to Do

Single or fixed-pane windows are much easier to replace than windows that are really one very large sheet of glass separated by snap-on grids, so keep that in mind when you begin replacing the glass.

 You will need to measure the length and width of the windowpane opening and subtract 1/16 of an inch from the dimensions. You can buy glass cut to size at a hardware store or home center. Make sure it's the same thickness as the glass you're replacing.

To replace the glass pane, you'll first need to clean out all of the broken glass from the sash. You may need to use a wood chisel to remove shards and old window glazing. Glazing can become quite brittle over time, but will soften up if you hold a blow dryer or heat gun over it for a bit. You can then chip it off.

Take the new pane of glass and insert it into the frame, bottom edge first. A groove called a rabbet runs through the inside of the window frame. The glass fits in there. Use the points to anchor the glass into the wood frame—you may need to use a hammer to make them stick into the wood.

Take window glazing, which is very much like Silly Putty, soften it in your hands and roll it into several long strings. Press the glazing around the edges of the pane into the rabbet of the frame, getting as close to the corners as possible. Then take a putty knife and smooth the glazing.

Clean the glass and allow the glazing to dry. Then prime and paint the glazing to match the paint on the frame.

Dead Car Battery

You and your kids just got home from a shopping trip, and your groceries are melting rapidly. You hop out of the car and begin shuttling bags into the kitchen. Your son lingers in the car, listening to his favorite song on the radio. You remind him to turn off the radio when he comes in and he assures you that not only will he remember, he's insulted that you'd think he'd forget. Duh.

The next morning you're late to get the kids to school. You herd them out of the house, pile everyone into the car, turn the key—and hear nothing but a sad "click." The radio wasn't turned off, and now the battery's dead. Your son is trying to hide in the back seat, and you're a very unhappy parent. Your car battery needs immediate CPR.

Here's What You Need

Jumper cables

A working car with access to its battery

Here's What to Do

You'll need another car and a set of jumper cables to resuscitate your vehicle.

1 Bring the working car's hood as close to your own as possible without touching your own, so that the jumper cables will reach both engine blocks. Turn off both cars, set both parking brakes, and open the hoods.

2 Find the positive (marked with a + or POS) and negative (marked with a – or NEG) posts on each battery. (Some new-model cars have dedicated jumper points, so if you have a new car, check your manual before proceeding.)

3 Attach the cable with the red clamps to the positive posts of each battery, and DO NOT let the red and black clamps of the jumper cables touch each other.

4 Attach the cable with the black clamps to the negative post on the car with the good battery. Attach the cable with the black clamps to the bare metal frame of the car with the dead battery so it is grounded—be sure you're not attaching it to the rubber gasket around the engine, since rubber is an insulator. DO NOT attach this clamp to the negative post of the dead battery, and make sure the cable isn't near the fan or fan belt of the car.

5 Start the car with the good battery and rev it a bit to make sure the battery is charged. Now try to start the car with the dead battery—it should start right up. If it doesn't after a couple more tries, there is probably something else wrong with it (lucky you), and you'll need to call a mechanic.

6 Keep both cars running and disconnect the cables, beginning with the black one that is being used as the ground and then the black one attached to the live battery. Again, don't let the red and black clamps touch each other.

7 Make sure you keep your car running for at least 15 minutes to help recharge the battery.

> ### Warning!
> *While most people will tell you they know how to jump start a car, make sure they really do before allowing them to do it for you. There's no sense in ruining two cars at once.*

De-Railed Bicycle Chain

You and your kids are off on a great bike ride, miles from your house. As you head up a slight hill, enjoying the feeling of being like one of those families in a breakfast cereal commercial, your daughter's bike makes an odd clacking noise, the pedals jam, and she falls right over. Turns out the chain has slipped off its cogs and your daughter won't be going anywhere without some quick roadside repair work. Otherwise, it's going to be a long walk home.

Here's What You Need

Lubrication oil for chain

Here's What to Do

Bike chains need to be replaced from front to back, since the rear cogs (or "chainrings") are what control the chain tension.

1 Prop the bike up against something supportive, like a tree, with the chain facing you.

2 Look for the small pulley wheels below the rear chainrings that have the chain looped through them.

3 Grab the (usually) polished frame of the bottom-most pulley with your left hand and push it toward the front of the bike so that the chain goes visibly slack.

4 Keeping the pulley pushed forward, use your right hand to grab the chain at its forward-most position, and place it onto the smallest chainring in the front. If the chain is very tight, you might need to wiggle it back and forth to get it on.

5 Once the chain is back on the ring, slowly ease the rear pulleys back to their natural position. The chain should be on both the front and rear cogs now.

6 If you have any chain lubrication (available at any sporting goods store), drip a few drops on the chain. The movement of the chain around the drivetrain will spread these few drops over the whole chain. Too much lube just collects dirt.

7 Lifting the back tire off the ground with your left hand, spin the pedals forward with your right hand to get the chain back in position. After a few clicks the chain should move smoothly around the cogs, and your daughter will be back in business.

Big Spill in the Car

You just went to the grocery store, and you've enlisted all the kids to help unload the car. They are working like little ants, scuttling back and forth with bags of groceries while you put them away in the house, when you suddenly hear, "Mom! Come quick! The milk's spilled!"

You race to the car to see a lake of milk slowly seeping into the carpeting on the car floor. It's a warm day, and you're pretty sure that it's not going to be a lot of fun to ride in that car in a couple of hours. You imagine what it will be like to drive in a sour milk mobile, and jump into action.

Here's What You Need

Towels

White vinegar

Water

Baking soda or cat litter

Shop vac or wet & dry vac, if available

Air fresheners shaped like evergreen trees

Here's What to Do

Immediately sop up as much milk as you can from the car floor with towels. You'll probably have to go through several towels, depending on how much milk spilled. If you have a shop vac or vacuum that can absorb liquid, fire it up and suck up as much milk as possible.

When you've blotted up as much standing liquid as possible, mix together a vinegar and water solution of two parts water to one part vinegar and scrub the wet spot. This will help neutralize the smell and alleviate stains.

Let the area dry. If you notice a smell like dirty feet (or worse), wash the area with the vinegar and water solution again. The smell may linger.

To make the air in the car more bearable, place a small, open container of baking soda or cat litter under the seat. Cat litter works as well as baking soda, and if it spills, can be brushed out. Baking soda, on the other hand, can be made into a paste and applied directly to the smell, then vacuumed off.

Interesting Tip

You may want to keep a few of those dangling evergreen tree-shaped air fresheners around the car for a while, especially if you live in a warm climate, or you leave your car out in the sun with the windows closed a lot.

Be Prepared

Stock these items at home and you'll be prepared for almost anything.

Hydrogen Peroxide

Why: It cleans up lots of different stains, from grape juice to dog poop, and it's a great disinfectant for small cuts and scrapes.

Spray Bottle

Why: Sometimes a little liquid goes a long way.

White vinegar & Baking soda

Why: White vinegar is an effective cleaner and smell remover, and when combined with baking soda makes a great mini volcano and/or a terrific dishwasher detergent substitute.

Ammonia

Why: It helps get the smell out of stains, especially pet-induced ones. Remember to never mix it with bleach: the combination can be deadly.

Nail polish remover

Why: The acetone in nail polish remover can break down the bonds of virtually any glue, paint or finish—not to mention nail polish.

Spackling compound

Why: They just don't make walls like they used to.

White glue

Why: For minor repairs, getting out splinters, and crafty projects

Duct tape

Why: What can't you fix with duct tape?

Basic Toolkit including:

Hammer
Toilet snake
Screwdrivers (phillips and flathead)
Adjustable locking pliers
Tape measure
Various screws, nails, tacks, and mollies

All-Purpose Disaster Kit

Carry these in your car wherever you go, and you'll never regret it.

Duct Tape

Why: It'll patch small or temporary holes in virtually anything from innertubes to backpacks, can be used to make anything from a drinking cup to a wallet, will keep a diaper on when the diaper tapes have either broken or lost their stickiness, and even remove splinters if you're desperate enough.

WD-40®

Why: It works as a universal solvent for anything stuck to skin, including superglue, marker, and chewing gum; it'll help remove any wax-based stain, including crayons, makeup, and candle spills; and it's great for polishing the inside of your car and lubricating your bike chain. (Incidentally, WD-40 stands for "Water Displacement—fortieth attempt.")

Dental Floss and Needle

Why: It is an ideal combination for making very durable repairs on ripped items (as long as you don't care how they look), including nylon bags, screens, car upholstery, and shoes. It is much more rugged than ordinary thread, and keeps your teeth and gums healthy, too.

Tweezers

Why: It's surprising the number of things you may need to pluck, including items lost in small places, money in the dashboard, splinters, etc.

Towel

Why: It's great for sopping up anything from kids who get soaked unexpectedly to a dog that rolls in dead stuff.

Cat Litter

Why: It not only absorbs unpleasant smells and soaks up spills, but if you get stuck in snow or ice you can throw it under the wheels of your car for better traction.

Plastic Garbage Bag

Why: It can be used as clothing, luggage, an emergency water bottle (when combined with a fair amount of duct tape), a seat cover for things you don't want to come in contact with your car upholstery, and finally, for trash.

Multi-purpose Utility Tool

Why: It can do anything—you'll feel like McGuyver.

Folding shovel

Why: It can really get you out of a jam if you're stuck in the mud or snow, and it folds up tiny enough to fit in the smallest trunk.

Resources and Acknowledgments:

While many of the techniques and solutions provided in this book are a result of many, many (usually unpleasant) instances of hands-on trial and error experience, thanks are necessary to the following companies and institutions that provided information and reassurance:

• Binney & Smith, a division of Hallmark Cards, Inc. for information about the Crayola Color Census.

• University of Missouri–Columbia Extension Service for information about stain removal from washable fabrics.

• Noise Pollution Clearinghouse for information about decibel levels and the human ear.

• University of Arkansas publications department for information about the discovery of ancient humans using toothpicks.

• www.bradyworld.com for information about The Brady Bunch.

• www.toiletpaperworld.com for statistics about consumer usage of toilet paper.

• Wm. Wrigley Jr. Company for information about the ingredients in chewing gum.

- Car Care Council in Port Clinton, OH, for guidelines about jump starting a car battery.

- University Medical Center in Tucson, AZ for information about how to remove cactus spines from skin.

- Professional Servicers Organization of California for information about the consequences of putting liquid soap in the dishwasher.

- Marshall Brain at www.howstuffworks.com for information about moths and their attraction to light.

- National Retail Hardware Association for information about how to create a drywall patch.

- United States Patent Office for information about Patent 1,219,881, the first zipper.

- Sanford Corporation for information about removing permanent marker from a variety of surfaces.

- www.Physlink.com, for information about microwaves.

- United States Golf Association for statistics about golf ball standards.

And many thanks to the following people:

- Denise Perkins, owner of Planet Hair, for information about how to remove petroleum jelly and chewing gum from hair.

- Lisa Fagan, jewelry maker, for information on repairing porcelain and other ceramics.

- Eric Goldwarg, bike repair expert, for information about replacing a bike chain.

- Leslie Connolly for information on how to remove a moth from an ear, and other anecdotes of disaster and repair.

- Joshua Kahan, handy man, for many hands-on lessons in toilet maintenance, repair, and removal.

- Rachel Benoit, Bruce Leasure, David Morin, Mark Schiffman, Jeff McAllister, Susan Hale, and Alex Kahan at Nomad Press, for their extraordinary ideas, skills, and patience.

- Anna Typrowicz for her impeccable editing skills.

- Charlie Woglom at Big Hed Designs for his terrific illustrations.

- Richard, Anastasia, Noah, and Simon for disasters every day of the week.

Disasters Notes:

About the Author

Lauri Berkenkamp has a master's degree in English Literature from the University of Vermont and is a former faculty member of Vermont College of Norwich University in Montpelier, Vermont. She has spent the last several years writing about the lighter side of parenting, and says her children ensure she's never lacking for material or opportunities to learn new skills—including picking locks, counteracting the effects of superglue, and making graceful apologies.